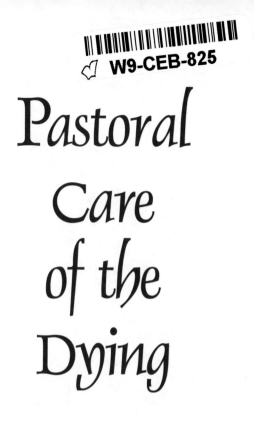

Pastoral

Care

of the

Dying

United States Conference of Catholic Bishops
Washington, D.C.

Concordat cum originali:
  Msgr. James Patrick Moroney
  Executive Director, Secretariat for the Liturgy
  United States Conference of Catholic Bishops

ISBN 1-57455-487-5

First Printing, August 2002

Contents

Foreword

Cast your care upon the LORD,
who will give you support.
God will never allow
the righteous one to stumble. (Ps 55:23)

Four years ago, as if he were standing with us by the bed of those whom we seek to commend to God, Pope John Paul II recalled these words from Psalm 55, as well as St. Augustine's reflections on them:

> What will you worry about? What will you be anxious for? He who made you will take care of you. Will he who took care of you before you came into being not take care of you now, when you are what he wanted you to be? . . . Abandon yourself to him; do not think that you are about to fall into the void; do not imagine such a thing. He has said: "I will fill the heavens and the earth." He will never fail you; do not fail him; do not fail yourself.[1]

With St. Augustine, our aging Holy Father, and all the saints and angels, we are called to stand beside the bed of those who are about to die, urging them

---

1 *Enarr. in Psalmos* 39, 26, 27: CCL 38, 445.

to greater faith, commending them to God's mercy, and tearfully placing them into God's hands.

A Word for You

You, dear reader, are probably about to take on that great work. Be strong; trust in God who seeks to console; shepherd and act through your words and hands.

Perhaps you are a priest. You have celebrated these rites many times. Once again you are called to be a vessel through which Christ, the one Eternal Priest, can refresh this dying man or woman, joining him or her to his eternal *sacrificium laudis* upon the cross.

Perhaps you are a deacon—after the priest, the first among all the ministers due to your conformity to Christ the suffering servant. As an ordained minister, your presence "shows more clearly that the Christian dies in the communion of the Church."[2]

Perhaps you are a lay chaplain or a lay pastoral minister. May Christ use the skills and gentle care with which he has graced you to bring comfort and healing and peace.

---

2 *Pastoral Care of the Sick: Rites of Anointing and Viaticum* (PCS) (New York: Catholic Book Publishing, 1983), no. 213.

Perhaps you are a friend or a relative of this dying person. You may be uncertain of what to do at a moment like this. Know that every Christian, from St. Peter to you, has felt the uncertainty and the fear of this moment. Through these prayers, and through you, Christ seeks to bring the sure and certain hope of his resurrection to this moment. Through these prayers, and through you, he walks again into the upper room that is locked with fear and says, "Peace be with you!"

These Rites of Final Commendation

The last prayers the Church prays for the dying person is what this booklet is all about. They may be led by a priest, a deacon, or any baptized person. Before leading or praying these prayers, you might want to read the Introduction for the Commendation of the Dying (nos. 212-216), which tells us that we may freely select from the prayers, which are best prayed "in a slow, quiet voice, alternating with periods of silence," (no. 214) with the dying person, with those gathered, or in one voice.

The first part of the Commendation of the Dying consists of short texts from the Sacred Scriptures or an invocation of the Blessed Virgin or St. Joseph. Each of these short prayers are eloquent beyond their brevity and seek to speak the deepest desires of our soul, couched in the silence of a moment when ordinary words fail us.

The second part of the Commendation of the Dying consists of longer readings from Sacred Scripture that in the words of Job, the Psalmist, and the Lord Jesus himself bring comfort and hope.

A special form of the Litany of the Saints begins the third part of these prayers and is followed by five different forms of the Prayer of Commendation, to be used when the moment of death seems near (no. 220). Like most of the prayers of final commendation, the first of these prayers has been prayed from the earliest days of the Church (*Go forth, Christian soul, from this world . . .*). Imagine the countless deathbeds around which Christians have tearfully prayed these words of faith before you!

The last section of the Commendation of the Dying provides prayers after death and prayers for families and friends, which may be appropriate in those sad, certain moments immediately after a person has returned to the God who gave him or her to us.

The Rites of Christian Dying

Hopefully, the dying person for whom you pray has had a chance to go to confession and receive the Sacrament of Penance, to be anointed, and to frequently receive Holy Communion in the course of his or her illness.

The last sacrament the dying person should receive is the Eucharist, Holy Viaticum. This "last Eucharist" may be administered by a priest, a deacon, or even, in their absence, an extraordinary minister of Holy Communion. They will use the rites[3] prescribed by the Church in bringing this food for the journey. These rites comprise the second part of this book.

Prayers for the Dead

The third part of this book contains prayers for ministers to use when attending a person who has already died.

Some Last Words

These are not easy prayers or rites to celebrate, but they are true and good and are at the heart of who we are as followers of Christ who has died, who is risen, and who will come again in glory! It may

---

3 PCS, nos. 197ff.

also help to know that you are not alone. Remember the words of the old Irish prayer inscribed on the wall of the chapel of Mary, Queen of Ireland, in the Basilica of the National Shrine of the Immaculate Conception in Washington, D.C.:

Holy Mary,
if thou wilt hear thy suppliant;
I put myself under the shelter of thy shield.
When falling in the slippery path,
thou art my smooth supporting hand staff.

There is no hound in fleetness or in chase,
north wind or rapid river,
as quick as the Mother of Christ
to the Bed of Death
of those who are entitled to her kindly
protection.

Join your prayers with hers, and know that she and all the saints and angels—gathered around Christ himself, whose saving death gives us hope—are here by this bed with you. Join your prayers with theirs, and you will find peace and your beloved dying brother or sister will find eternal rest in God.

Msgr. James Patrick Moroney
Executive Director
USCCB Secretariat for the Liturgy

Introduction

When we were baptized in Christ Jesus we were baptized into his death . . . so that as Christ was raised from the dead by the Father's glory, we too might live a new life.

161 The[se] rites . . . are used by the Church to comfort and strengthen a dying Christian in the passage from this life. The ministry to the dying places emphasis on trust in the Lord's promise of eternal life rather than on the struggle against illness which is characteristic of the pastoral care of the sick. . . .

[142]

162 Priests with pastoral responsibilities are to direct the efforts of the family and friends as well as other ministers of the local Church in the care of the dying. They should ensure that all are familiar with the rites provided here.

The words "priest," "deacon," and "minister" are used advisedly. Only in those rites which must be celebrated by a priest is the word "priest" used in the rubrics (that is, the sacrament of penance, the sacrament of the anointing of the sick, the celebration of viaticum within Mass). Whenever it is clear that, in the absence of a priest, a deacon may preside at a particular rite, the words "priest or deacon" are used in the rubrics. Whenever another minister is permitted to celebrate a rite in the absence of a priest or deacon, the word "minister" is used in the rubrics, even though in many cases the rite will be celebrated by a priest or deacon.

[138]

163 The Christian community has a continuing responsibility to pray for and with the person who is dying. Through its sacramental ministry to the dying the community helps Christians to embrace death in mysterious union with the crucified and risen Lord, who awaits them in the fullness of life.

Celebration of Viaticum [94]

164 A rite . . . for viaticum outside Mass [is] provided. If possible, viaticum should take place within the full eucharistic celebration, with the family, friends, and other members of the Christian community taking part. The rite for viaticum outside Mass is used when the full eucharistic celebration cannot take place. Again, if it is possible, others should take part.

Commendation of the Dying

165 [This book] . . . contains a collection of prayers for the spiritual comfort of the Christian who is close to death. These prayers are traditionally called the commendation of the dying to God and are to be used according to the circumstances of each case.

Prayers for the Dead

166 A chapter has also been provided to assist a minister who has been called to attend a person who is already dead. A priest is not to administer the sacrament of anointing. Instead, he should pray for the dead person, using prayers such as those which appear in this [book]. He may find it necessary to explain to the family of the person who is dead that sacraments are celebrated for the living, not for the dead, and that the dead are effectively helped by the prayers of the living.

Care of a Dying Child

168* In its ministry to the dying the Church must also respond to the difficult circumstances of a dying child. Although no specific rites appear in [this book] . . . for the care of a dying child, these notes are provided to help bring into focus the various aspects of this ministry.

---

* Paragraph no. 167 omitted.

169 When parents learn that their child is dying, they are often bewildered and hurt. In their love for their son or daughter, they may be beset by temptations and doubts and find themselves asking: Why is God taking this child from us? How have we sinned or failed that God would punish us in this way? Why is this innocent child being hurt?

Under these trying circumstances, much of the Church's ministry will be directed to the parents and family. While pain and suffering in an innocent child are difficult for others to bear, the Church helps the parents and family to accept what God has allowed to happen. It should be understood by all beforehand that this process of acceptance will probably extend beyond the death of the child. The concern of the Christian community should continue as long as necessary.

Concern for the child must be equal to that for the family. Those who deal with dying children observe that their faith matures rapidly. Though young children often seem to accept death more easily than adults, they will often experience a surprisingly mature anguish because of the pain which they see in their families.

170 At such a time, it is important for members of the Christian community to come to the support

of the child and the family by prayer, visits, and other forms of assistance. Those who have lost children of their own have a ministry of consolation and support to the family. Hospital personnel (doctors, nurses, aides) should also be prepared to exercise a special role with the child as caring adults. Priests and deacons bear particular responsibility for overseeing all these elements of the Church's pastoral ministry. The minister should invite members of the community to use their individual gifts in this work of communal care and concern.

171   By conversation and brief services of readings and prayers, the minister may help the parents and family to see that their child is being called ahead of them to enter the kingdom and joy of the Lord. The period when the child is dying can become a special time of renewal and prayer for the family and close friends. The minister should help them to see that the child's sufferings are united to those of Jesus for the salvation of the whole world.

172   If it is appropriate, the priest should discuss with the parents the possibility of preparing and celebrating with the child the sacraments of initiation (baptism, confirmation, eucharist). The priest may baptize and confirm the child. . . . To

complete the process of initiation, the child should also receive first communion.

According to the circumstances, some of these rites may be celebrated by a deacon or lay person. So that the child and family may receive full benefit from them, these rites are normally celebrated over a period of time. In this case, the minister should use the usual rites, that is, the *Rite of Baptism for Children*, the *Rite of Confirmation*, and if suitable, the *Rite of Penance*. Similarly, if time allows, the usual rites for anointing and viaticum should be celebrated.

173 If sudden illness or an accident has placed an unitiated child in proximate danger of death, the minister uses "Christian Initiation for the Dying," . . . adapting it for use with a child.

174 For an initiated child or a child lacking only the sacrament of confirmation, who is in proximate danger of death, the "Continuous Rite of Penance, Anointing, and Viaticum" . . . may be used and adapted to the understanding of the child. If death is imminent it should be remembered that viaticum rather than anointing is the sacrament for the dying.*

---

* See pp. 53-76 for subsequent paragraphs for the rite for viaticum outside Mass.

Commendation of the Dying

INTRODUCTION

Into your hands, Lord, I commend my spirit.

212 In viaticum the dying person is united with Christ in his passage out of this world to the Father. Through the prayers for the commendation of the dying contained in this [section], the Church helps to sustain this union until it is brought to fulfillment after death.

[138, 142]

213 Christians have the responsibility of expressing their union in Christ by joining the dying person in prayer for God's mercy and for confidence in Christ. In particular, the presence of a priest or deacon shows more clearly that the Christian dies in the communion of the Church. He should assist the dying person and those present in the recitation of the prayers of commendation and, following death, he should

lead those present in the prayer after death. If the priest or deacon is unable to be present because of other serious pastoral obligations, other members of the community should be prepared to assist with these prayers and should have the texts readily available to them.

[139, 140]

214 The minister may choose texts from among the prayers, litanies, aspirations, psalms, and readings provided in this [section], or others may be added. In the selection of these texts the minister should keep in mind the condition and piety of both the dying person and the members of the family who are present. The prayers are best said in a slow, quiet voice, alternating with periods of silence. If possible, the minister says one or more of the brief prayer formulas with the dying person. These may be softly repeated two or three times.

[139]

215 These texts are intended to help the dying person, if still conscious, to face the natural human anxiety about death by imitating Christ in his patient suffering and dying. The Christian will be helped to surmount his or her fear in the hope of heavenly life and resurrection through the power of Christ, who destroyed the power of death by his own dying.

Even if the dying person is not conscious, those who are present will draw consolation from these prayers and come to a better understanding of the paschal character of Christian death. This may be visibly expressed by making the sign of the cross on the forehead of the dying person, who was first signed with the cross at baptism.

[141]

216 Immediately after death has occurred, all may kneel while one of those present leads the prayers given on pp. 36-44.

COMMENDATION OF THE DYING

Short Texts

[140]

217 One or more of the following short texts may be recited with the dying person. If necessary, they may be softly repeated two or three times.

[143]

Who can separate us from the love of Christ?

Romans 8:35

Whether we live or die, we are the Lord's.

Romans 14:8

We have an everlasting home in heaven.

2 Corinthians 5:1

We shall be with the Lord for ever.

1 Thessalonians 4:17

We shall see God as he really is.

1 John 3:2

**We have passed from death to life
because we love each other.**

1 John 3:14

To you, Lord, I lift up my soul.

Psalm 25:1

The Lord is my light and my salvation.

Psalm 27:1

**I believe that I shall see the goodness
of the Lord in the land of the living.**

Psalm 27:13

My soul thirsts for the living God.

Psalm 42:3

Though I walk in the shadow of death,
I will fear no evil,
for you are with me.

Psalm 23:4

Come, blessed of my Father,
says the Lord Jesus,
and take possession of the kingdom
prepared for you.

Matthew 25:34

The Lord Jesus says,
today you will be with me in paradise.

Luke 23:43

In my Father's home
there are many dwelling places,
says the Lord Jesus.

John 14:2

The Lord Jesus says,
I go to prepare a place for you,
and I will come again to take you
   to myself.

John 14:2-3

I desire that where I am,
they also may be with me,
says the Lord Jesus.

John 17:24

**Everyone who believes in the Son
has eternal life.**

John 6:40

**Into your hands, Lord,
I commend my spirit.**

Psalm 31:5a

Lord Jesus, receive my spirit.

Acts 7:59

Holy Mary, pray for me.

Saint Joseph, pray for me.

**Jesus, Mary, and Joseph,
assist me in my last agony.**

READING   [144]
218 The word of God is proclaimed by one of
those present or by the minister. Selections from
. . . the following readings may be used:

A   Job 19:23-27
*Job's act of faith is a model for our own; God
is the God of the living.*

12

Job said:
Oh, would that my words were written down!
  Would that they were inscribed in a record:
That with an iron chisel and with lead
  they were cut in the rock forever!

But as for me, I know that my Vindicator lives,
  and that he will at last stand forth upon
    the dust;
Whom I myself shall see:
  my own eyes, not another's, shall
    behold him.
And from my flesh I shall see God;
  my inmost being is consumed with longing.

This is the Word of the Lord.

B   Psalm 23
The Lord is my shepherd; I shall not want.
  In verdant pastures he gives me repose;
Beside restful waters he leads me;
  he refreshes my soul.

He guides me in right paths
  for his name's sake.
Even though I walk in the dark valley
  I fear no evil; for you are at my side
With your rod and your staff
  that give me courage.

You spread the table before me
    in the sight of my foes;
You anoint my head with oil;
    my cup overflows.

Only goodness and kindness follow me
    all the days of my life;
And I shall dwell in the house of the Lord
    for years to come.

C   Psalm 25

To you I lift up my soul,
    O Lord, my God.
Your ways, O Lord, make known to me;
    teach me your paths,
Guide me in your truth and teach me,
    for you are God my savior,
    and for you I wait all the day.

Remember that your compassion, O Lord,
    and your kindness are from of old.
The sins of my youth and my frailties
  remember not;
    in your kindness remember me,
    because of your goodness, O Lord.

Good and upright is the Lord;
　　thus he shows sinners the way.
He guides the humble to justice,
　　he teaches the humble his way.

All the paths of the Lord are kindness
　　and constancy
　　　　toward those who keep his covenant
　　　　　　and his decrees.
For your name's sake, O Lord,
　　you will pardon my guilt, great as it is.

D　　　　　　　　　　　　　　　　　　Psalm 91

You who dwell in the shelter of the Most High,
　　who abide in the shadow of the Almighty,
Say to the Lord, "My refuge and my fortress,
　　my God, in whom I trust."
For he will rescue you from the snare of
　　the fowler,
　　　　from the destroying pestilence.
With his pinions he will cover you,
　　and under his wings you shall take refuge;
　　his faithfulness is a buckler and a shield.

You shall not fear the terror of the night
　　nor the arrow that flies by day;
Not the pestilence that roams in darkness
　　nor the devastating plague at noon.

Though a thousand fall at your side,
  ten thousand at your right side,
  near you it shall not come.
Rather with your eyes shall you behold
  and see the requital of the wicked,
Because you have the Lord for your refuge;
  you have made the Most High your
    stronghold.

No evil shall befall you,
  nor shall affliction come near your tent,
For to his angels he has given command
  about you,
  that they guard you in all your ways.
Upon their hands they shall bear you up,
  lest you dash your foot against a stone.

You shall tread upon the asp and the viper;
  you shall trample down the lion and
    the dragon.
Because he clings to me, I will deliver him;
  I will set him on high because he
    acknowledges my name.
He shall call upon me, and I will answer him;
  I will be with him in distress;
I will deliver him and glorify him;
  with length of days I will gratify him
  and will show him my salvation.

E

I lift up my eyes toward the mountains;
    whence shall help come to me?
My help is from the Lord,
    who made heaven and earth.

May he not suffer your foot to slip;
    may he slumber not who guards you:
Indeed he neither slumbers nor sleeps,
    the guardian of Israel.

The Lord is your guardian; the Lord is
  your shade;
    he is beside you at your right hand.
The Lord will guard you from all evil;
    he will guard your life.
The Lord will guard your coming and
  your going,
    both now and forever.

F 1 John 4:16

We have come to know and to believe
in the love God has for us.
God is love,
and he who abides in love
abides in God,
and God in him.

G

God our Father is the God of newness and life; it is his desire that we should come to share his life with him.

I, John, saw new heavens and a new earth. The former heavens and the former earth had passed away, and the sea was no longer. I also saw a new Jerusalem, the holy city, coming down out of heaven from God, beautiful as a bride prepared to meet her husband. I heard a loud voice from the throne cry out: "This is God's dwelling among men. He shall dwell with them and they shall be his people, and he shall be their God who is always with them. He shall wipe every tear from their eyes, and there shall be no more death or mourning, crying out or pain, for the former world has passed away."

The One who sat on the throne said to me, "See, I make all things new! I am the Alpha and the Omega, the Beginning and the End. To anyone who thirsts I will give to drink without cost from the spring of life-giving water. He who wins the victory shall inherit these gifts; I will be his God and he shall be my son."

Jesus bids us be prepared for our ultimate destiny, which is eternal life.

[Jesus told his disciples this parable:] "The reign of God can be likened to ten bridesmaids who took their torches and went out to welcome the groom. Five of them were foolish, while the other five were sensible. The foolish ones, in taking their torches, brought no oil along, but the sensible ones took flasks of oil as well as their torches. The groom delayed his coming, so they all began to nod, then to fall asleep. At midnight someone shouted, 'The groom is here! Come out and greet him!'

"At the outcry all the virgins woke up and got their torches ready. The foolish ones said to the sensible, 'Give us some of your oil. Our torches are going out.' But the sensible ones replied, 'No, there may not be enough for you and us. You had better go to the dealers and buy yourselves some.' While they went off to buy it the groom arrived, and the ones who were ready went in to the wedding with him. Then the door was barred. Later the other bridesmaids came back. 'Master, master!' they cried. 'Open the door for us.' But he answered, 'I tell you, I do not know you.'

"The moral is: keep your eyes open, for you know not the day or the hour."

I   Luke 22:39-46
Jesus is alive to our pain and sorrow, because faithfulness to his Father's will cost him his life itself.

Jesus went out and made his way, as was his custom, to the Mount of Olives; his disciples accompanied him. On reaching the place he said to them, "Pray that you may not be put to the test."

He withdrew from them about a stone's throw, then went down on his knees and prayed in these words: "Father, if it is your will, take this cup from me; yet not my will but yours be done." An angel then appeared to him from heaven to strengthen him. In his anguish he prayed with all the greater intensity, and his sweat became like drops of blood falling to the ground.

Then he rose from prayer and came to his disciples, only to find them asleep, exhausted with grief. He said to them, "Why are you sleeping? Wake up, and pray that you may not be subjected to the trial."

J Luke 23:44-49

Jesus' death is witnessed by his friends.

It was now around midday, and darkness came over the whole land until midafternoon with an eclipse of the sun. The curtain in the sanctuary was torn in two. Jesus uttered a loud cry and said,

"Father, into your hands I commend my spirit." After he said this, he expired.

The centurion, upon seeing what had happened, gave glory to God by saying, "Surely this was an innocent man." When the crowd which had assembled for this spectacle saw what had happened, they went home beating their breasts.

All his friends and the women who had accompanied him from Galilee were standing at a distance watching everything.

K Luke 24:1-8

Jesus is alive; he gives us eternal life with the Father.

On the first day of the week, at dawn, the women came to the tomb bringing the spices they had prepared. They found the stone rolled back from the tomb; but when they entered the tomb, they did not find the body of the Lord Jesus. While they were still at a loss over what to think of this, two men in dazzling garments appeared beside them. Terrified, the women bowed to the ground.

The men said to them: "Why do you search for the living One among the dead? He is not here; he has been raised up. Remember what he said to you while he was still in Galilee— that the Son of Man must be delivered into the hands of sinful men, and be crucified, and on the third day rise again." With this reminder, his words came back to them.

L   John 6:37-40
Jesus will raise his own from death and give them eternal life.

Jesus says:

"All that the Father gives me shall come to me; no one who comes will I ever reject, because it is not to do my own will that I have come down from heaven, but to do the will of him who sent me.

It is the will of him who sent me
that I should lose nothing of what he has
   given me;
rather, that I should raise it up on the last day.
Indeed, this is the will of my Father,
that everyone who looks upon the Son
and believes in him
shall have eternal life.
Him I will raise up on the last day."

M   John 14:1-6, 23, 27
The love of Jesus can raise us up from the
sorrow of death to the joy of eternal life.

Jesus says:

"Do not let your hearts be troubled.
Have faith in God
and faith in me.
In my Father's house there are many
   dwelling places;
otherwise, how could I have told you
that I was going to prepare a place for you?
I am indeed going to prepare a place
   for you,
and then I shall come back to take you
   with me,
that where I am you also may be.
You know the way that leads where I go."

"Lord," said Thomas, "we do not know where you are going. How can we know the way?" Jesus told him:

> "I am the way, and the truth, and the life;
> no one comes to the Father but
>   through me.

> "Anyone who loves me
> will be true to my word,
> and my Father will love him;
> we will come to him
> and make our dwelling place with him.

> "'Peace' is my farewell to you,
> my peace is my gift to you;
> I do not give it to you as the world
>   gives peace.
> Do not be distressed or fearful."

Litany of the Saints [145]

219 When the condition of the dying person calls for the use of brief forms of prayer, those who are present are encouraged to pray the litany of the saints—or at least some of its invocations—for him or her. Special mention may be made of the patron saints of the dying person, of the family, and of the parish. The litany may be

said or sung in the usual way. Other customary prayers may also be used.

One of the following litanies may be used:

A

Lord, have mercy

                Lord, have mercy

Christ, have mercy

                Christ, have mercy

Lord, have mercy

                Lord, have mercy

Holy Mary, Mother of God

                pray for him/her

Holy angels of God

                pray for him/her

Abraham, our father in faith

                pray for him/her

David, leader of God's people

                pray for him/her

All holy patriarchs and prophets

                pray for him/her

Saint John the Baptist

                pray for him/her

Saint Joseph

                pray for him/her

Saint Peter and Saint Paul

                pray for him/her

Saint Andrew

> pray for him/her

Saint John

> pray for him/her

Saint Mary Magdalene

> pray for him/her

Saint Stephen

> pray for him/her

Saint Ignatius

> pray for him/her

Saint Lawrence

> pray for him/her

Saint Perpetua and Saint Felicity

> pray for him/her

Saint Agnes

> pray for him/her

Saint Gregory

> pray for him/her

Saint Augustine

> pray for him/her

Saint Athanasius

> pray for him/her

Saint Basil

> pray for him/her

Saint Martin

> pray for him/her

Saint Benedict

> pray for him/her

Saint Francis and Saint Dominic

> pray for him/her

Saint Francis Xavier

> pray for him/her

Saint John Vianney

> pray for him/her

Saint Catherine

> pray for him/her

Saint Teresa

> pray for him/her

Other saints may be included here.

All holy men and women

> pray for him/her

Lord, be merciful

> Lord, save your people

From all evil

> Lord, save your people

From every sin

> Lord, save your people

From Satan's power

> Lord, save your people

At the moment of death

> Lord, save your people

From everlasting death

> Lord, save your people

On the day of judgment

> Lord, save your people

By your coming as man

> Lord, save your people

By your suffering and cross
> Lord, save your people

By your death and rising to new life
> Lord, save your people

By your return in glory to the Father
> Lord, save your people

By your gift of the Holy Spirit
> Lord, save your people

By your coming again in glory
> Lord, save your people

Be merciful to us sinners
> Lord, hear our prayer

Bring N. to eternal life, first promised to him/her in baptism
> Lord, hear our prayer

Raise N. on the last day, for he/she has eaten the bread of life
> Lord, hear our prayer

Let N. share in your glory, for he/she has shared in your suffering and death
> Lord, hear our prayer

Jesus, Son of the living God
> Lord, hear our prayer

Christ, hear us
> Christ, hear us

Lord Jesus, hear our prayer
> Lord Jesus, hear our prayer

B

A brief form of the litany may be prayed. Other saints may be added, including the patron saints of the dying person, of the family, and of the parish; saints to whom the dying person may have a special devotion may also be included.

Holy Mary, Mother of God

pray for him/her

Holy angels of God

pray for him/her

Saint John the Baptist

pray for him/her

Saint Joseph

pray for him/her

Saint Peter and Saint Paul

pray for him/her

Other saints may be included here.

All holy men and women

pray for him/her

Prayer of Commendation [145]

220 When the moment of death seems near, some of the following prayers may be said:

A [146]

Go forth, Christian soul, from this world
in the name of God the almighty Father,
who created you,
in the name of Jesus Christ, Son of the
   living God,
who suffered for you,
in the name of the Holy Spirit,
who was poured out upon you,
go forth, faithful Christian.

May you live in peace this day,
may your home be with God in Zion,
with Mary, the virgin Mother of God,
with Joseph, and all the angels and saints.

B [147]

I commend you, my dear brother/sister, to
   almighty God,
and entrust you to your Creator.
May you return to him
who formed you from the dust of the earth.
May holy Mary, the angels, and all the saints
come to meet you as you go forth from
   this life.
May Christ who was crucified for you
bring you freedom and peace.
May Christ who died for you
admit you into his garden of paradise.

May Christ, the true Shepherd,
acknowledge you as one of his flock.
May he forgive all your sins,
and set you among those he has chosen.
May you see your Redeemer face to face,
and enjoy the vision of God for ever.

R/. Amen.

C [148]

Welcome your servant, Lord, into the place of
salvation which because of your mercy he/she
rightly hoped for.

R/. Amen, or R/. Lord, save your people.

Deliver your servant, Lord, from every distress.

R/. Amen, or R/. Lord, save your people.

Deliver your servant, Lord, as you delivered
Noah from the flood.

R/. Amen, or R/. Lord, save your people.

Deliver your servant, Lord, as you delivered
Abraham from Ur of the Chaldees.

R/. Amen, or R/. Lord, save your people.

31

Deliver your servant, Lord, as you delivered
Job from his sufferings.

R/. Amen, or R/. Lord, save your people.

Deliver your servant, Lord, as you delivered
Moses from the hand of the Pharaoh.

R/. Amen, or R/. Lord, save your people.

Deliver your servant, Lord, as you delivered
Daniel from the den of lions.

R/. Amen, or R/. Lord, save your people.

Deliver your servant, Lord, as you delivered
the three young men from the fiery furnace.

R/. Amen, or R/. Lord, save your people.

Deliver your servant, Lord, as you delivered
Susanna from her false accusers.

R/. Amen, or R/. Lord, save your people.

Deliver your servant, Lord, as you delivered
David from the attacks of Saul and Goliath.

R/. Amen, or R/. Lord, save your people.

Deliver your servant, Lord, as you delivered Peter and Paul from prison.

R̸. Amen, or R̸. Lord, save your people.

Deliver your servant, Lord, through Jesus our Savior, who suffered death for us and gave us eternal life.

R̸. Amen, or R̸. Lord, save your people.

D [149]

Lord Jesus Christ, Savior of the world,
we pray for your servant N.,
and commend him/her to your mercy.
For his/her sake you came down
   from heaven;
receive him/her now into the joy of
   your kingdom.

For though he/she has sinned,
he/she has not denied the Father, the Son,
   and the Holy Spirit,
but has believed in God
and has worshiped his/her Creator.

R̸. Amen.

E [150]

The following antiphon may be said or sung:

Hail, holy Queen, Mother of mercy,
hail, our life, our sweetness, and our hope.
To you we cry, the children of Eve;
to you we send up our sighs,
mourning and weeping in this land of exile.
Turn, then, most gracious advocate,
your eyes of mercy toward us;
lead us home at last
and show us the blessed fruit of your
   womb, Jesus:
O clement, O loving, O sweet Virgin Mary.

Prayer After Death [151]

221   When death has occurred, one or more of
the following prayers may be said:

A

Saints of God, come to his/her aid!
Come to meet him/her, angels of the Lord!

> ℟. Receive his/her soul and present
> him/her to God the Most High.

May Christ, who called you, take you
  to himself;
may angels lead you to Abraham's side.

R̷. Receive his/her soul and present
him/her to God the Most High.

Give him/her eternal rest, O Lord,
and may your light shine on him/her for ever.

R̷. Receive his/her soul and present
him/her to God the Most High.

The following prayer is added:

Let us pray.

All-powerful and merciful God,
we commend to you N., your servant.
In your mercy and love,
blot out the sins he/she has committed
  through human weakness.
In this world he/she had died:
let him/her live with you for ever.

We ask this through Christ our Lord.

R̷. Amen.

B [F163]

Psalm 130

    ℟. My soul hopes in the Lord.

Out of the depths I cry to you, O Lord;
    Lord, hear my voice!
Let your ears be attentive
    to my voice in supplication.

    ℟. My soul hopes in the Lord.

I trust in the Lord;
    my soul trusts in his word.
My soul waits for the Lord
    more than sentinels wait for the dawn.

    ℟. My soul hopes in the Lord.

For with the Lord is kindness
    and with him is plenteous redemption;
And he will redeem Israel
    from all their iniquities.

    ℟. My soul hopes in the Lord.

[F30]

The following prayer is added:

Let us pray.

God of love,
welcome into your presence
your son/daughter N., whom you have called
   from this life.
Release him/her from all his/her sins,
bless him/her with eternal light and peace,
raise him/her up to live for ever with all
   your saints
in the glory of the resurrection.

We ask this through Christ our Lord.

   ℟. Amen.

C   [F145]
Psalm 23
   ℟. Lord, remember me in your kingdom.

The Lord is my shepherd; I shall not want.
   In verdant pastures he gives me repose;
Beside restful waters he leads me;
   he refreshes my soul.

   ℟. Lord, remember me in your kingdom.

He guides me in right paths
    for his name's sake.
Even though I walk in the dark valley
    I fear no evil; for you are at my side
With your rod and your staff
    that give me courage.

    ℟. Lord, remember me in your kingdom.

You spread the table before me
    in the sight of my foes;
You anoint my head with oil;
    my cup overflows.

    ℟. Lord, remember me in your kingdom.

Only goodness and kindness follow me
    all the days of my life;
And I shall dwell in the house of the Lord
    for years to come.

    ℟. Lord, remember me in your kingdom.

[F33]

The following prayer is added:

Let us pray.

God of mercy,
hear our prayers and be merciful
to your son/daughter N., whom you have
    called from this life.
Welcome him/her into the company of
    your saints,
in the kingdom of light and peace.

We ask this through Christ our Lord.

    ℟. Amen.

D   [F167]
Almighty and eternal God,
hear our prayers for your son/daughter N.,
whom you have called from this life
    to yourself.

Grant him/her light, happiness, and peace.
Let him/her pass in safety through the gates
    of death,
and live for ever with all your saints
in the light you promised to Abraham
and to all his descendants in faith.

Guard him/her from all harm
and on that great day of resurrection
  and reward
raise him/her up with all your saints.
Pardon his/her sins
and give him/her eternal life in your kingdom.

We ask this through Christ our Lord.

  R/. Amen.

E [F168]

Loving and merciful God,
we entrust our brother/sister to your mercy.

You loved him/her greatly in this life:
now that he/she is freed from all its cares,
give him/her happiness and peace for ever.

The old order has passed away:
welcome him/her now into paradise
where there will be no more sorrow,
no more weeping or pain,
but only peace and joy
with Jesus, your Son,
and the Holy Spirit
for ever and ever.

  R/. Amen.

F

God of our destiny,
into your hands we commend our
   brother/sister.
We are confident that with all who have died
   in Christ
he/she will be raised to life on the last day
and live with Christ for ever.

[We thank you for all the blessings
you gave him/her in this life
to show your fatherly care for all of us
and the fellowship which is ours with the saints
in Jesus Christ.]

Lord, hear our prayer:
welcome our brother/sister to paradise
and help us to comfort each other
with the assurance of our faith
until we all meet in Christ
to be with you and with our brother/sister
   for ever.
We ask this through Christ our Lord.

   ℟. Amen.

Prayer for the Family and Friends

222   One of the following prayers may be said:

Let us pray.

A   [F34]

For the family and friends

God of all consolation,
in your unending love and mercy for us
you turn the darkness of death
into the dawn of new life.
Show compassion to your people in
   their sorrow.

[Be our refuge and our strength
to lift us from the darkness of this grief
to the peace and light of your presence.]

Your Son, our Lord Jesus Christ,
by dying for us, conquered death
and by rising again, restored life.

May we then go forward eagerly to meet him,
and after our life on earth
be reunited with our brothers and sisters
where every tear will be wiped away.

We ask this through Christ our Lord.

R/. Amen.

B [F169]
For the deceased person and for the family and
friends

Lord Jesus, our Redeemer,
you willingly gave yourself up to death
so that all people might be saved
and pass from death into a new life.
Listen to our prayers,
look with love on your people
who mourn and pray for their brother/sister N.

Lord Jesus, holy and compassionate:
forgive N. his/her sins.
By dying you opened the gates of life
for those who believe in you:

do not let our brother/sister be parted
   from you,
but by your glorious power
give him/her light, joy, and peace in heaven
where you live for ever and ever.

  ℟. Amen.

For the solace of those present the minister may conclude these prayers with a simple blessing or with a symbolic gesture, for example, signing the forehead with the sign of the cross. A priest or deacon may sprinkle the body with holy water.

Celebration of Viaticum

INTRODUCTION

I am going to prepare a place for you; I shall come back and take you with me.

175   This chapter contains a rite for . . . viaticum outside Mass. The celebration of the eucharist as viaticum, food for the passage through death to eternal life, is the sacrament proper to the dying Christian. It is the completion and crown of the Christian life on this earth, signifying that the Christian follows the Lord to eternal glory and the banquet of the heavenly kingdom.

The sacrament of the anointing of the sick should be celebrated at the beginning of a serious illness. Viaticum, celebrated when death is close, will then be better understood as the last sacrament of Christian life.

[93]

176   Priests and other ministers entrusted with the spiritual care of the sick should do everything they

45

can to ensure that those in proximate danger of death receive the body and blood of Christ as viaticum. At the earliest opportunity, the necessary preparation should be given to the dying person, family, and others who may take part.

[26, 101]

177   Whenever it is possible, the dying Christian should be able to receive viaticum within Mass. In this way he or she shares fully, during the final moments of this life, in the eucharistic sacrifice, which proclaims the Lord's own passing through death to life. However, circumstances, such as confinement to a hospital ward or the very emergency which makes death imminent, may fre-quently make the complete eucharistic celebration impossible. In this case, the rite for viaticum outside Mass is appropriate. The minister should wear attire appropriate to this ministry.

178   Because the celebration of viaticum ordinarily takes place in the limited circumstances of the home, a hospital, or other institution, the simplifications of the rite for Masses in small gatherings may be appropriate. Depending on the condition of the dying person, every effort should be made to involve him or her, the family, friends, and other members of the local community in the planning and celebration. Appropriate readings, prayers, and songs will help to foster the full

participation of all. Because of this concern for participation, the minister should ensure that viaticum is celebrated while the dying person is still able to take part and respond.

[28,108]
179 A distinctive feature of the celebration of viaticum, whether within or outside Mass, is the renewal of the baptismal profession of faith by the dying person. This occurs after the homily and replaces the usual form of the profession of faith. Through the baptismal profession at the end of earthly life, the one who is dying uses the language of his or her initial commitment, which is renewed each Easter and on other occasions in the Christian life. In the context of viaticum, it is a renewal and fulfillment of initiation into the Christian mysteries, baptism leading to the eucharist.

[99d, 114]
180 The rites for viaticum within and outside Mass may include the sign of peace. The minister and all who are present embrace the dying Christian. In this and in other parts of the celebration the sense of leave-taking need not be concealed or denied, but the joy of Christian hope, which is the comfort and strength of the one near death, should also be evident.

181   As an indication that the reception of the eucharist by the dying Christian is a pledge of resurrection and food for the passage through death, the special words proper to viaticum are added: "May the Lord Jesus Christ protect you and lead you to eternal life." The dying person and all who are present may receive communion under both kinds. The sign of communion is more complete when received in this manner because it expresses more fully and clearly the nature of the eucharist as a meal, one which prepares all who take part in it for the heavenly banquet. . . .

The minister should choose the manner of giving communion under both kinds which is suitable in the particular case. If the wine is consecrated at a Mass not celebrated in the presence of the sick person, the blood of the Lord is kept in a properly covered vessel and is placed in the tabernacle after communion. The precious blood should be carried to the sick person in a vessel which is closed in such a way as to eliminate all danger of spilling. If some of the precious blood remains after communion, it should be consumed by the minister, who should also see to it that the vessel is properly purified.

The sick who are unable to receive under the form of bread may receive under the form of wine alone. If the wine is consecrated at a Mass not celebrated in the presence of the sick person, the instructions given above are followed.

182 In addition to these elements of the rites which are to be given greater stress, special texts are provided for the general intercessions or litany and the final solemn blessing.

183 It often happens that a person who has received the eucharist as viaticum lingers in a grave condition or at the point of death for a period of days or longer. In these circumstances he or she should be given the opportunity to receive the eucharist as viaticum on successive days, frequently if not daily. This may take place during or outside Mass as particular conditions permit. The rite may be simplified according to the condition of the one who is dying.

Viaticum Outside Mass

186* Although viaticum celebrated in the context of the full eucharistic celebration is always preferable, when it is not possible the rite for viaticum outside Mass is appropriate. This rite includes some of the elements of the Mass, especially a brief liturgy of the word. Depending on the circumstances and the condition of the

---

* Paragraph nos. 184-185 omitted.

dying person, this rite should also be a communal celebration. Every effort should be made to involve the dying person, family, friends, and members of the local community in the planning and celebration. The manner of celebration and the elements of the rite which are used should be accommodated to those present and the nearness of death.

[100]

187   If the dying person wishes to celebrate the sacrament of penance and this cannot take place during a previous visit, it should be celebrated before the rite of viaticum begins, especially if others are present. Alternatively, it may be celebrated during the rite of viaticum, replacing the penitential rite. At the discretion of the priest, the apostolic pardon may be added after the penitential rite or after the sacrament of penance.

[107]

188   An abbreviated liturgy of the word, ordinarily consisting of a single biblical reading, gives the minister an opportunity to explain the word of God in relation to viaticum. The sacrament should be described as the sacred food which strengthens the Christian for the passage through death to life in sure hope of the resurrection.

VIATICUM OUTSIDE MASS

Introductory Rites

GREETING

[101]

197* The minister greets the sick person and the others present. One of the following may be used:

A

The peace of the Lord be with you always.

R/. And also with you.

B

Peace be with you (this house) and with all who live here.

R/. And also with you.

C   [230]

The grace of our Lord Jesus Christ and the love of God and the fellowship of the Holy Spirit be with you all.

R/. And also with you.

---

* Paragraph nos. 189-196 omitted.

D [231]

The grace and peace of God our Father and the Lord Jesus Christ be with you.

R̶. And also with you.

[101]

The minister then places the blessed sacrament on the table, and all join in adoration.

SPRINKLING WITH HOLY WATER

[102]

198 If it seems desirable, the priest or deacon may sprinkle the sick person and those present with holy water. One of the following may be used:

A

Let this water call to mind our baptism into Christ, who by his death and resurrection has redeemed us.

B

The Lord is our shepherd
and leads us to streams of living water.

INSTRUCTION

[103]

199 Afterward the minister addresses those present, using the following instruction or one better suited to the sick person's condition.

My brothers and sisters, before our Lord Jesus Christ passed from this world to return to the Father, he left us the sacrament of his body and blood. When the hour comes for us to pass from this life and join him, he strengthens us with this food for our journey and comforts us by this pledge of our resurrection.

[104]

If the sacrament of penance is now celebrated . . . the penitential rite is omitted. In case of necessity, this may be a generic confession.

PENITENTIAL RITE

[105]

200 The minister invites the sick person and all present to join in the penitential rite, using these or similar words:

A

My brothers and sisters, to prepare ourselves for this celebration, let us call to mind our sins.

B

My brothers and sisters, let us turn with confidence to the Lord and ask his forgiveness for all our sins.

[105]

After a brief period of silence, the penitential rite continues, using one of the following:

A

All say:

> I confess to almighty God,
> and to you, my brothers and sisters,
> that I have sinned through my own fault
>   They strike their breast.
> in my thoughts and in my words,
> in what I have done,
> and in what I have failed to do;
> and I ask blessed Mary, ever virgin,
> all the angels and saints,
> and you, my brothers and sisters,
> to pray for me to the Lord our God.

B

By your paschal mystery you have won for
  us salvation:
Lord, have mercy.

    ℟. Lord, have mercy.

You renew among us now the wonders of
  your passion:
Christ, have mercy.

    ℟. Christ, have mercy.

When we receive your body,
you share with us your paschal sacrifice:
Lord, have mercy.

    ℟. Lord, have mercy.

[105]

The minister concludes the penitential rite with
the following:

May almighty God have mercy on us,
forgive us our sins,
and bring us to everlasting life.

    ℟. Amen.

Apostolic Pardon

[106]

201 At the conclusion of the sacrament of penance or the penitential rite, the priest may give the apostolic pardon for the dying, using one of the following:

A

Through the holy mysteries of
  our redemption,
may almighty God release you from
  all punishments
in this life and in the life to come.

May he open to you the gates of paradise
and welcome you to everlasting joy.

R∕. Amen.

B

By the authority which the Apostolic See has
  given me,
I grant you a full pardon and the remission
  of all your sins
in the name of the Father, and of the Son, †
  and of the Holy Spirit.

R∕. Amen.

Liturgy of the Word

READING

[107]

202   The word of God is proclaimed by one of those present or by the minister. An appropriate reading from . . . one of the following readings may be used:

A

> † A reading from the holy gospel
> according to John 6:54-55

Jesus says:
"He who feeds on my flesh
and drinks my blood
has life eternal,
and I will raise him up on the last day.
For my flesh is real food
and my blood real drink."

This is the Gospel of the Lord.

B

† A reading from the holy gospel
according to John 14:23

Jesus says:
"Anyone who loves me
will be true to my word,
and my Father will love him;
we will come to him
and make our dwelling place with him."

This is the Gospel of the Lord.

C

† A reading from the holy gospel
according to John 15:4

Jesus says:
"Live on in me, as I do in you.
No more than a branch can bear fruit
  of itself
apart from the vine,
can you bear fruit
apart from me."

This is the Gospel of the Lord.

D

A reading from the first letter of Paul to the Corinthians 11:26

Every time, then, you eat this bread and drink this cup, you proclaim the death of the Lord until he comes!

This is the Word of the Lord.

HOMILY

[107]

203   Depending on circumstances, the minister may then give a brief explanation of the reading.

BAPTISMAL PROFESSION OF FAITH

[108]

204   It is desirable that the sick person renew his or her baptismal profession of faith before receiving viaticum. The minister gives a brief introduction and then asks the following questions:

N., do you believe in God, the
  Father almighty,
creator of heaven and earth?

  ℟. I do.

Do you believe in Jesus Christ, his only Son,
  our Lord,
who was born of the Virgin Mary,
was crucified, died, and was buried,
rose from the dead,
and is now seated at the right hand of
  the Father?

℞. I do.

Do you believe in the Holy Spirit,
the holy catholic Church, the communion
  of saints,
the forgiveness of sins, the resurrection of
  the body,
and life everlasting?

℞. I do.

LITANY

[109]

205   The minister may adapt or shorten the litany
according to the condition of the sick person. The
litany may be omitted if the sick person has made
the profession of faith and appears to be tiring.

My brothers and sisters, with one heart let us
call on our Savior Jesus Christ.

You loved us to the very end and gave yourself over to death in order to give us life. For our brother/sister, Lord, we pray:

℟. Lord, hear our prayer.

You said to us: "All who eat my flesh and drink my blood will live for ever." For our brother/sister, Lord, we pray:

℟. Lord, hear our prayer.

You invite us to join in the banquet where pain and sorrow, sadness and separation will be no more. For our brother/sister, Lord, we pray:

℟. Lord, hear our prayer.

Liturgy of Viaticum

THE LORD'S PRAYER

[110]

206 The minister introduces the Lord's Prayer in these or similar words:

A

Now let us offer together the prayer our Lord Jesus Christ taught us:

B

And now let us pray with confidence as Christ our Lord commanded:

All say:

Our Father . . .

COMMUNION AS VIATICUM

[99e]

207　The sick person and all present may receive communion under both kinds. When the minister gives communion to the sick person, the form for viaticum is used.

[111]

The minister shows the eucharistic bread to those present, saying:

A

Jesus Christ is the food for our journey;
he calls us to the heavenly table.

B

This is the bread of life.
Taste and see that the Lord is good.

The sick person and all who are to receive communion say:

> Lord, I am not worthy to receive you,
> but only say the word and I shall
>   be healed.

The minister goes to the sick person and, showing the blessed sacrament, says:

The body of Christ.

The sick person answers: "Amen."

Then the minister says:

The blood of Christ.

The sick person answers: "Amen."

Immediately, or after giving communion to the sick person, the minister adds:

May the Lord Jesus Christ protect you and lead you to eternal life.

> R̸. Amen.

Others present who wish to receive communion then do so in the usual way.

[113]

After the conclusion of the rite, the minister cleanses the vessel as usual.

SILENT PRAYER

[113]

208   Then a period of silence may be observed.

PRAYER AFTER COMMUNION

[114]

209   The minister says a concluding prayer. One of the following may be used:

Let us pray.

Pause for silent prayer, if this has not preceded.

A   [259]

God of peace,
you offer eternal healing to those who believe
**   in you;**
you have refreshed your servant N.
with food and drink from heaven:
lead him/her safely into the kingdom of light.

We ask this through Christ our Lord.

R/. Amen.

B   [57]
All-powerful and ever-living God,
may the body and blood of Christ your Son
be for our brother/sister N.
a lasting remedy for body and soul.

We ask this through Christ our Lord.

R/. Amen.

C   [114]
Father,
your Son, Jesus Christ, is our way, our truth,
    and our life.
Look with compassion on your servant N.
who has trusted in your promises.
You have refreshed him/her with the body
    and blood of your Son:
may he/she enter your kingdom in peace.

We ask this through Christ our Lord.

R/. Amen.

Concluding Rites

BLESSING

[114]

210   The priest or deacon blesses the sick person and the others present, using one of the following blessings. If, however, any of the blessed sacrament remains, he may bless the sick person by making a sign of the cross with the blessed sacrament, in silence.

A [237]

May the Lord be with you to protect you.

R/. Amen.

May the Lord guide you and give you strength.

R/. Amen.

May the Lord watch over you, keep you in his care, and bless you with his peace.

R/. Amen.

May almighty God bless you,
the Father, and the Son, † and the Holy Spirit.

℞. Amen.

B [79]

May God the Father bless you.

℞. Amen.

May God the Son comfort you.

℞. Amen.

May God the Holy Spirit enlighten you.

℞. Amen.

May almighty God bless you,
the Father, and the Son, † and the Holy Spirit.

℞. Amen.

C [238]

May the blessing of almighty God,
the Father, and the Son, † and the Holy Spirit,
come upon you and remain with you for ever.

℞. Amen.

A minister who is not a priest or deacon invokes God's blessing and makes the sign of the cross on himself or herself, while saying:

A

May the Lord bless us,
protect us from all evil,
and bring us to everlasting life.

R̸. Amen

B

May the almighty and merciful God bless and
protect us, the Father, and the Son, and the
Holy Spirit.

R̸. Amen

SIGN OF PEACE

[114]

211   The minister and the others present may then give the sick person the sign of peace.

Prayers for the Dead

INTRODUCTION

I want those you have given me to be with me where I am.

[15]

223 This chapter contains prayers for use by a minister who has been called to attend a person who is already dead. A priest is not to administer the sacraments of penance or anointing. Instead, he should pray for the dead person using these or similar prayers.

224 It may be necessary to explain to the family of the person who is dead that sacraments are celebrated for the living, not for the dead, and that the dead are effectively helped by the prayers of the living.

225 To comfort those present the minister may conclude these prayers with a simple blessing or with a symbolic gesture, for example, making the sign of the cross on the forehead. A priest or deacon may sprinkle the body with holy water.

PRAYERS FOR THE DEAD

Greeting

226 The minister greets those who are present, offering them sympathy and the consolation of faith, using one of the following or similar words:

A

In this moment of sorrow
the Lord is in our midst
and comforts us with his word:
Blessed are the sorrowful; they shall
  be consoled.

B

Praised be God, the Father of our Lord
  Jesus Christ,
the Father of mercies,
and the God of all consolation!
He comforts us in all our afflictions
and thus enables us to comfort those who are
  in trouble,
with the same consolation
we have received from him.

Prayer

227 The minister then says one of the following prayers, commending the person who has just died to God's mercy and goodness:

Let us pray.

A

Almighty and eternal God,
hear our prayers for your son/daughter N.,
whom you have called from this life
   to yourself.

Grant him/her light, happiness, and peace.
Let him/her pass in safety through the gates
   of death,
and live for ever with all your saints
in the light you promised to Abraham
and to all his descendants in faith.
Guard him/her from all harm
and on that great day of resurrection
   and reward
raise him/her up with all your saints.
Pardon his/her sins
and give him/her eternal life in your kingdom.

We ask this through Christ our Lord.

℞. Amen

B

Loving and merciful God,
we entrust our brother/sister to your mercy.

You loved him/her greatly in this life:
now that he/she is freed from all its cares,
give him/her happiness and peace for ever.

The old order has passed away:
welcome him/her now into paradise
where there will be no more sorrow,
no more weeping or pain,
but only peace and joy
with Jesus, your Son,
and the Holy Spirit
for ever and ever.

℟. Amen

Reading

228 The word of God is proclaimed by one of those present or by the minister. An appropriate reading from one of the following readings may be used:

A

† A reading from the holy gospel
according to Luke 23:44-46

It was now around midday, and darkness came over the whole land until midafternoon with an eclipse of the sun. The curtain in the sanctuary was torn in two. Jesus uttered a loud cry and said,

"Father, into your hand I commend
my spirit."

After he said this, he expired.

This is the Gospel of the Lord.

B

† A reading from the holy gospel
according to John 11:3-7, 17,
20-27, 33-36, 41-44

This sisters sent word to Jesus to inform
him, "Lord, the one you love is sick." Upon
hearing this, Jesus said:

"The sickness is not to end in death;
rather it is for God's glory,
that through it the Son of God may be
glorified."

Jesus loved Martha and her sister and Lazarus
very much. Yet, after hearing that Lazarus was
sick, he stayed on where he was for two days
more. Finally he said to his disciples, "Let us
go back to Judea."

When Jesus arrived at Bethany, he found that
Lazarus had already been in the tomb four
days. When Martha heard that Jesus was
coming she went to meet him, while Mary sat
at home. Martha said to Jesus, "Lord, if you
had been here, my brother would never have

died. Even now, I am sure that God will give you whatever you ask of him." "Your brother will rise again," Jesus assured her. "I know he will rise again," Martha replied, "in the resurrection on the last day." Jesus told her:

"I am the resurrection and the life:
whoever believes in me,
though he should die, will come to life;
and whoever is alive and believes in me
will never die.

"Do you believe this?" "Yes, Lord," she replied. "I have come to believe that you are the Messiah, the Son of God: he who is come into the world."

When Jesus saw her weeping, and the Jews who had accompanied her also weeping, he was troubled in spirit, moved by the deepest emotions. "Where have you laid him?" he asked. "Lord, come and see," they said. Jesus began to weep, which caused the Jews to remark, "See how much he loved him!"

The Jesus looked upward and said:

"Father, I thank you for having heard me.
I know that you always hear me

but I have said this for the sake of
the crowd,
that they may believe that you sent me."

Having said this he called loudly, "Lazarus, come out!" The dead man came out, bound hand and foot with linen strips, his face wrapped in a cloth. "Untie him," Jesus told them, "and let him go free."

This is the Gospel of the Lord.

Litany

229 Then one of those present may lead the others in praying a brief form of the litany of the saints. (The full form of the litany of the saints may be found on p. 24.) Other saints may be added, including the patron saints of the dead person, of the family, and of the parish; saints to whom the deceased person may have had a special devotion may also be included.

Saints of God, come to his/her aid!
Come to meet him/her, angels of the Lord!

Holy Mary, Mother of God   pray for him/her
Saint Joseph   pray for him/her
Saint Peter and Saint Paul   pray for him/her

The following prayer is added:

God of mercy,
hear our prayers and be merciful
to your son/daughter N., whom you have
  called from this life.
Welcome him/her into the company of
  your saints,
in the kingdom of light and peace.
We ask this through Christ our Lord.

R/. Amen

The Lord's Prayer

230 The minister introduces the Lord's Prayer in these or similar words:

A

With God there is mercy and fullness of redemption; let us pray as Jesus taught us to pray:

B

Let us pray for the coming of the kingdom as Jesus taught us:

All say:

Our Father . . .

Prayer of Commendation [F169]

231 The minister then concludes with the following prayer:

Lord Jesus, our Redeemer,
you willingly gave yourself up to death
so that all people might be saved
and pass from death into a new life.
Listen to our prayers,
look with love on your people
who mourn and pray for their
  brother/sister N.

Lord Jesus, holy and compassionate:
forgive N. his/her sins.
By dying you opened the gates of life
for those who believe in you:
do not let our brother/sister be parted
  from you,
but by your glorious power
give him/her light, joy, and peace in heaven
where you live for ever and ever.

R/. Amen

For the solace of those present the minister may conclude these prayers with a simple blessing or with a symbolic gesture, for example, signing the forehead with the sign of the cross. A priest or deacon may sprinkle the body with holy water.

To order this resource or to obtain a catalog of other USCCB titles, call toll-free 800-235-8722. In the Washington metropolitan area or from outside the United States, call 202-722-8716. Visit the U.S. bishops' Internet site located at www.usccb.org.